BE
HEALED

God's Promises
and Encouragement
for Your Total
Well-Being

Contents

3   Introduction

4   Healing Is God's Will

14   Instant Miracles vs. Progressive Healing

26   Healing in the Old Testament

38   Jesus and Healing in the New Testament

48   Healing for Physical Sickness

58   Healing for Broken Relationships

68   Healing for the Mind

78   Healing for Stress

88   Healing for Depression

98   Healing for Guilt, Shame, and Condemnation

108   Healing When You've Been Hurt

118   Healing for Someone You Love

Have a story of healing? We'd love to hear it! Visit TBN.org/MyStory or post on social media using the hashtag #MyStory.

INTRODUCTION

When it comes to your life, God left nothing to chance. He gave you His Word to cover every circumstance or situation you might ever encounter. Not only did He give you His Word, but He also made a covenant with you—a covenant that ensures that every promise you read in Scripture is, from His perspective, a settled issue.

God doesn't want you wondering whether or not *all* His promises are for you. They are! And that includes His promises about health and healing.

From Genesis to Revelation, there's concrete evidence of God's healing power. Scripture is full of His promises about healing, as well as testimonies of miraculous healing taking place. Both in the Old and New Testaments, there is no question that healing has always been on God's mind. He wants His people well!

Why then is there still doubt in the body of Christ as to whether or not God is willing to heal His people? In many cases, this doubt stems from stories of Believers who didn't receive their healing.

But God never told us to base our faith on other people's experiences. We are instructed to put our trust in Him and the absolute truth of His Word alone— a Word that trumps any experience an individual might have.

Let this devotional be a testament of God's eternal and unconditional love for you. Let it remind you of His healing promises. More importantly, let it be unshakable evidence to you of His will *for you* to be healed and whole. Allow the Scriptures, faith affirmations, real-life partner testimonies, and insights from some of your favorite ministers encourage you and strengthen your faith.

Receive the life within these pages and know, beyond the shadow of a doubt, *it is God's will for you to* **Be Healed!**

CHAPTER 1

HEALING IS GOD'S WILL

Healing is God's will.

There's no question about it! It's important to settle this truth in our hearts because while God has already made up His mind on the subject, we must set our faith in agreement with Him.

God never intended us to go through life doubting His intentions. That's why He graciously gave us His Word. During His ministry on Earth, Jesus ran into doubt about God's promises time and again. A leper who knew His power to heal and deliver sheepishly began his healing request with, "Lord, *if* you are willing … " The leper knew Jesus *could* heal him, but he doubted whether Jesus *would* heal him. Jesus cleared up this doubt with three simple words: "I am willing." And then He said, "Be healed!" (Matthew 8:2–3, NLT) The Bible records that the leprosy disappeared *instantly.*

As seen in this account, it's one thing to have head-knowledge of God's healing power … it's another to have settled within ourselves that healing is the will of God. Even today. For each of us. It is God's will for you to be healed!

How serious is God about healing? 1 Peter 2:24 makes
it abundantly clear. <u>God is so serious about healing that
He directly connected it to Jesus' death on the cross.</u>
Jesus' brutal chastisement and crucifixion is the ultimate
expression of God's love for you. He took upon Himself
every wound, or "stripe," so you wouldn't have to bear
it yourself. Yes, your healing is a direct result of Christ's
loving sacrifice. We don't ever doubt Christ's triumph
over death at the cross, or our salvation because of it.
Why would we ever doubt the Father's will to heal?

Now, take it one step further. Pay close attention to the
verb tense in this Scripture. It says, "By whose stripes you
were healed." That's *past tense.* From God's perspective, if
you are a Believer in Christ, *He already sees you as healed!*

If you are facing persistent symptoms, it can be easy to doubt
and wonder if God wants to heal you. But that's why God gave
us promises like the one in 1 Peter 2:24. We no longer have
to wonder if it's God's will to heal. It *is.* Just as sure as Jesus
died for us, He has bought us our healing. Once and for all.

... who Himself bore our sins in His own body on the tree,
that we, having died to sins, might live for righteousness—
by whose stripes you were healed. (1 Peter 2:24, NKJV)

GOD'S PROMISES

But he was pierced

for our rebellion,

crushed for our sins. He

was beaten so we could

be whole. He was whipped

so we could be healed.

(ISAIAH 53:5, NLT)

Jesus was ...

wounded and bruised for all of my sins and rebellion. The punishment needed in order for me to be made whole was placed upon Him. With the stripes, blows, and wounds He suffered, my healing was purchased. I am healed in Christ!

Let all that I am praise the LORD; may I never forget the good things he does for me. He forgives all my sins and heals all my diseases. He redeems me from death and crowns me with love and tender mercies. (Psalm 103:2-4, NLT)

I am grateful and remember all the good things God does for me. He has forgiven all my sin. He heals all sickness and disease. He has redeemed my life from destruction and danger. I am crowned with His love, mercy, and favor!

A vast crowd brought to him people who were lame, blind, crippled, those who couldn't speak, and many others. They laid them before Jesus, and he healed them all. (Matthew 15:30, NLT)

Jesus Christ is the same yesterday, today, and forever. (Hebrews 13:8, NLT)

Jesus is my healer. Healing has always been His will. He has not changed. He is eternally the same. I have a right to experience the same healing power as those in the Bible. He healed "them all," and that includes me! He is my healer.

HEALING NUGGETS

"Jesus can heal you everywhere you hurt. Jesus cares about every single part of you. He cares about your mind, your emotions, your physical body. I don't believe it's God best for you to constantly feel bad, have no energy, and be in pain all the time. Release your faith for God to heal you."
—JOYCE MEYER

"If God withholds your healing after He has already given you Jesus, then it would mean your healing is greater or more important than Jesus. No ... He has already given you heaven's best. How will He not also freely give you all things, including the healing and wholeness you desire?"
—JOSEPH PRINCE

"You combat thoughts with words. Thoughts have no power until they're spoken. So when the devil says you're not going to get your healing, say, 'Satan, by His stripes I was, I am healed now!'"
—KENNETH COPELAND

"I broke my knee in 2012. I did not have surgery because the doctor said it was shattered like a windshield and would heal in time. Over time it did heal and I could finally walk. But one day I was on the floor and could hardly get up. It was like it was broken all over again. I was in constant pain.

"[Not long after that] an old broadcast from 1985 with Paul Crouch and Oral Roberts was on TBN. Paul began to pray for sick people. The pain stopped! My knee is better than it's been since I broke it. I don't have a limp. God is still using Paul even now!"

—MOLLY HUMBIRD, TBN PARTNER

CHAPTER 2

INSTANT MIRACLES VS. PROGRESSIVE HEALING

The Word is clear ...

that healing is God's will, but many Believers don't realize that healing can take place in different ways. Sometimes God performs a miracle and instantly heals someone. Other times, God heals people over time.

When looking at Scripture and the many miracles Jesus performed in the Bible, it's easy to think He always heals people in the same fashion. But on closer examination, we see that in many cases He doesn't do the same thing twice.

For instance, here's how He healed the blind:

- In Matthew 9:29, Jesus healed two blind men by touching their eyes.
- In Mark 10:52, Jesus healed Bartimaeus by *speaking* rather than by touching him.
- In Mark 8:22–25, Jesus put spit on a blind man's eyes and laid hands on Him twice before he was completely healed.

Jesus wasn't bound to one method of healing people—but He was *always* willing. Regardless of the method, receivers consistently showed belief in His ability to heal and a willingness for Him to release His power on their behalf. The same is true today!

If you've prayed for healing and nothing happened immediately, that doesn't mean your faith faltered. It doesn't mean God is angry at you and wants you to suffer. It just means it's time to thank God that you are taking Him at His Word and getting better one day after another. It means accepting that what is already finished in the spirit realm is working itself into the physical realm.

Remember, from God's perspective, you are *already* healed in Christ!

So if you experience progressive healing
rather than an instant miracle ...

DON'T BE DISCOURAGED

Just because you didn't see instant results doesn't mean your
prayer wasn't answered. The Word of God is a seed and
is growing inside you progressively (Matthew 13:23).

God has given you the grace to hold on to what you
believe from the Word while it takes root and grows.

BE GRATEFUL

No matter what situation you find yourself in, it's always a good
time to be thankful. You may only have started the healing
process. But don't fall for the enemy's trick. He wants you to
focus on what appears unchanged, when you could be thanking
God for the part of your life that has gotten better. Thank God
you are getting better, stronger, and healthier day by day.

CONTINUE TO
FEED YOUR FAITH

As you are standing in faith and allowing the Word to work inside you, continue to meditate on the promises of God about healing. God's Word always works when you plant it in your heart. Keep watering that seed by continuing to speak God's healing promises over your life.

In Isaiah 55:10–11, God says, "The rain and snow come down from the heavens and stay on the ground to water the earth. They cause the grain to grow, producing seed for the farmer and bread for the hungry. It is the same with my word. I send it out, and it always produces fruit. It will accomplish all I want it to, and it will prosper everywhere I send it." (NLT)

GOD'S
PROMISES

... the one who sows to the Spirit

will from the Spirit reap eternal

life. Let us not grow weary or

become discouraged in doing

good, for at the proper time we

will reap, if we do not give in.

(GALATIANS 6:8-9, AMP)

I will continue

to sow the spiritual seed of God's Word in my life, and I will reap an abundant harvest. God helps me to stay the course. He keeps me from getting weary and giving up until I see the full healing that has already been given to me by Jesus.

Do not turn me over to the desire of my foes ... I remain confident of this: I will see the goodness of the LORD in the land of the living. Wait for the LORD; be strong and take heart and wait for the LORD. (Psalm 27:12–14, NIV)

CONFESSION:

God will not allow the enemies of sickness, pain, and disease to defeat me. The Holy Spirit in me helps me remain confident. I will see the goodness of the Lord. I wait upon the Lord by focusing on His promise to me, and I thank Him for my entire healing.

HEALING NUGGETS

"When you partake of the Lord's Supper, you are partaking of the Lord's health. Yet, don't always expect instantaneous manifestations when you do. This is a lifestyle. Just know every time you partake, even though you don't see immediate manifestation, you are getting better. The fact you remember Him, even though there's no immediate result, glorifies Him."
—JOSEPH PRINCE

"Someone asked me recently if I didn't think God was unfair, allowing me to have Parkinson's and other medical problems when I have tried to serve Him faithfully. I replied that I did not see it that way at all. Suffering is part of the human condition, and it comes to us all. The key is how we react to it, either turning away from God in anger and bitterness or growing closer to Him in trust and confidence."
—BILLY GRAHAM

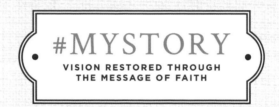

I needed a
miracle. I believe
the Lord touched
me that day.

After a catastrophic tornado, TBN Partner Shanda Tripp was trapped under a destroyed house.

"The rescuer—my Good Samaritan—pulled me out, and that was the last thing I saw. I later found out I had broken my ribs. The marrow in my bones released into my bloodstream and collected in my eyes as poison. I couldn't drive a car. I couldn't feed my children, and I COULD NOT read my Bible! That's when I developed such an appreciation for Christian television.

"I had TBN on constantly. I remember watching ... and I don't remember what the sermon was ... but when they were praying for the sick, whatever they said, I did it. I needed a miracle. I believe the Lord touched me that day.

"I kept hoping that I would wake up instantly with 20/20 vision. That didn't happen, but then slowly my vision began to come back! When I went to the seven-week checkup, I had 20/20 vision!

"When someone who believes God can come into your living room through television and pray with you—that is awesome. I can declare Jesus is a HEALER because TBN was there for me!"
—SHANDA TRIPP, TBN PARTNER

CHAPTER 3

HEALING IN THE OLD TESTAMENT

The subject of healing appears throughout the whole of Scripture.

From Genesis to Revelation, there is documented evidence of God's attitude toward sickness, pain, and disease. Many Believers don't realize the Old Testament is full of healing promises as well as documented examples of God healing people.

The Old Testament begins with God's original design for mankind. God never intended for mankind to die. This is why He lovingly instructed Adam and Eve to stay away from what would bring death. Spiritual death and all its effects—such as physical death, sickness, disease, and pain—were a result of sin. Those things were never God's will.

If you ever doubt God's willingness to heal, or are tempted to think He is using sickness as form of punishment to teach you a lesson, remember that from the very beginning eternal life, free from death and sickness, was always His plan.

As you journey through the Old Testament you'll come across stories like:

- God healing Naaman of leprosy (2 Kings 5:14–15)
- Elijah raising the widow's son from the dead (1 Kings 17:17–24)
- God healing Hannah's infertility (1 Samuel 1:19–20)
- The children of Israel being healed when bitten by poisonous snakes in the wilderness (Numbers 21:4–9)

The evidence is overwhelming that healing was always something God provided for His people, even after mankind sinned. But even beyond the healing of disease and sickness, the Old Testament provides evidence that God was also focused on the strength and sustained health of His people.

Our heavenly Father is not just focused on us receiving healing when illness comes. He is also concerned with us living in continual health and strength.

Look at what Psalm 105:37 says about the children of Israel when God delivered them from slavery in Egypt:

He brought them forth also with silver and gold: and there was not one feeble person among their tribes. (KJV)

The children of Israel did not leave Egypt weak and sick. They left strong and healthy. God is not just concerned with sickness or extreme disease; He wants to make sure you live a life of strength and vitality.

God didn't do more for the children of Israel under the Old Covenant than He has done for us in Christ. We must have confidence as we see the glory of God's healing power in the Old Testament, that the same power is still available for us to walk in today!

Our heavenly Father is not just focused on us receiving healing when illness comes. He is also concerned with us living in continual health and strength.

GOD'S PROMISES

He sent his word,

and healed them,

and delivered them

from their destructions.

(PSALM 107:20, KJV)

God has given me His Word.

His Word is the source of my continued health and healing. He has delivered me from all destruction. Even if I have made decisions that caused ill health in my life, God has forgiven me in Christ and delivers me continuously from all sickness, pain, weakness, and any disease.

Because you have made the LORD, who is my refuge, even the Most High, your dwelling place, no evil shall befall you, nor shall any plague come near your dwelling. (Psalm 91:9–10, NKJV)

CONFESSION:

God is my refuge and dwelling place. There is no sickness in His presence, and since I abide with Him, sickness cannot remain in my life. No disease, outbreak, virus, or illness can come near me and remain. I am protected in Christ.

... let the weak say, I am strong. (Joel 3:10, KJV)

CONFESSION:

I don't speak the language of weakness, sickness, or disease. I call myself strong even when I feel weak. I am healthy, strong, youthful, and vigorous in Christ.

Who satisfies your mouth [your necessity and desire at your personal age and situation] with good so that your youth, renewed, is like the eagle's [strong, overcoming, soaring]! (Psalm 103:5, AMPC)

CONFESSION:

Jesus is my source of complete satisfaction. My youth and strength are renewed. I age gracefully in Christ.

HEALING NUGGETS

"When you wake up in the morning say something about good about yourself. Words have creative power. They can bless you or curse you. Speak healing instead of sickness since life and death is in the power of the tongue."
—JOEL OSTEEN

"I can't heal you, and I'm not a healer, but I know One who is. His name is Jesus, and nothing is impossible with Him. Jesus can touch you and raise you up. You shall recover in Jesus' name."
—JENTEZEN FRANKLIN

"It is always God's will to heal us. We can be confident in determining God's will for healing by looking at the life of Jesus."
—CREFLO DOLLAR

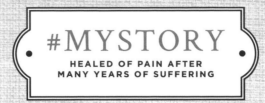

#MYSTORY

**HEALED OF PAIN AFTER
MANY YEARS OF SUFFERING**

"I had severe pain in my jaws, which caused me to have four jaw surgeries. Most of the time I was in pain and had migraine headaches almost every day. I had been prayed for many times over the years for jaw pain, migraines, and other health issues.

Eventually God brought to mind that I needed to receive His forgiveness for my sins. One time I was watching TBN, and Leon Fontaine was teaching. I prayed for healing with him. From that moment I have not had any pain in my jaws after having suffered for years."

—SHIRIA WHITTAKER, TBN PARTNER

CHAPTER 4

JESUS AND HEALING IN THE NEW TESTAMENT

Even with all ...

of the evidence in the Old Testament of God's will concerning healing, it doesn't stop there. With the New Testament, God has given you a better covenant based on better promises in Christ (Hebrews 8:6).

Maybe you find yourself doubting if it's God's will to heal you because of a longstanding illness or symptoms you've dealt with. If you find yourself in that circumstance, the best thing to do is to look at Jesus.

We don't have to stretch our imaginations to imagine what Jesus would do. We can just open the Bible. Look at all the stories in the Gospels of the numerous people Jesus healed, delivered from demonic possession, and raised from the dead. When we see Christ, we are seeing the Father's heart for us. Just simply reading about the many healings and miracles He performed on a continual basis will cause our expectation to rise.

And all the healings throughout the Gospels happened before Jesus died. He had not yet purchased salvation for the world or paid the price for sin.

Occasionally, the people Jesus ministered to were unsaved and were not even a part of the covenant He established with Israel.

Remember the story of the centurion who prayed for Jesus to heal his servant in Matthew 8? He was an unsaved outsider, and he received healing for his servant. He simply asked Jesus for healing, and he believed Jesus was willing and able to heal.

Throughout the Gospels, people with varying levels of sickness and disease went to Jesus for healing. There were people who were sick, and there were others who were near death. There were people who had strong faith, and there were others who struggled to believe. The key to every one of those miracles is that those people made sure they were in the presence of Jesus. Here are just some of the healings Jesus performed:

- Simon's mother healed of fever (Matthew 8:14–15)
- Resurrection of Jairus' daughter (Mark 5:21–24, 35–43)
- Healing of woman with the issue of blood (Mark 5:25–34)
- Healing of a deaf man (Mark 7:32–37)
- Healing of a severed ear (Luke 22:47–51)
- Healing of a blind man (John 9:1–41)

Take time to read through these documented testimonies and others … and boost your faith for your own health and well-being!

GOD'S PROMISES

Beloved, I pray that you

may prosper in all things

and be in health,

just as your soul prospers.

(3 JOHN 1:2, NKJV)

CONFESSION:

I declare that ...

because of Jesus I am successful in all things.
I am healthy in my mind, my emotions, my
relationships, and my physical body.

My child, pay attention to what I say. Listen carefully to my words. Don't lose sight of them. Let them penetrate deep into your heart, for they bring life to those who find them, and healing to their whole body. **(Proverbs 4:20–22, NLT)**

CONFESSION:

I remove distractions and put my focus on God's Word.
I receive His Word regularly, and His promises are alive inside
of me. His promises sustain my health, keep me disease-free,
and cause me to live in peace inwardly and outwardly.

*... and great multitudes followed him, and he
healed them all.* (Matthew 12:15, KJV)

CONFESSION:

Jesus is a healer. I am His sheep. I follow Him, and His
healing power permeates every area of my life.

HEALING NUGGETS

"Even if you are suffering with AIDS, Jesus can heal you. You may be outside the parameters of medical science, but you're not outside the reach of God."
—JOHN HAGEE

"You may be going through a rocky road right now, but the Lord wants you to know it's going to turn out all right. It might not feel good or look good right now, but it's going to turn out all right."
—T.D. JAKES

"In life there's going to be pain. In life there's going to be hurt. In life there's going to be sickness. That's why God makes it so abundantly clear to us in Scripture who He is. He is the Lord who heals you. Receive Him as your healer like you've received Him as your Savior."
—GREGORY DICKOW

We prayed
because the
prayers of
the righteous
avail much.

"When my mother got sick with cancer, I said, 'God, I do not accuse You in this moment. I understand John 10:10. It's the devil that comes to steal, kill, and destroy. You came that we may have life.' I said, 'Cancer, I refuse to allow you to sit on the throne of my emotions.' We prayed because the prayers of the righteous avail much.

"Eventually my mother went for surgery. It was supposed to last three hours. The day of, I got a phone call, and my aunt said, 'You aren't going to believe this. You know that cancer that was on her pancreas and liver with a 1.8% survival rate? It's not there! The lesions on her liver are gone! Her liver is perfect!' They searched all over, and they couldn't find any cancer. Why? Because there is nobody greater!"

—PASTOR JOHN GRAY, TBN MINISTRY PARTNER

CHAPTER 5

HEALING FOR PHYSICAL SICKNESS

If you're dealing with ...

physical sickness right now, believing for your healing, take hold of the promises throughout this devotional. Each one will help you stand firm on what God has promised and not settle for less than all Jesus died for you to have.

Or, you may also be reading because you simply want to have long-term health and strength in your body. You want to age gracefully and maintain vitality year after year. Regardless of your situation, there are scriptural promises just for you.

One of the most powerful verses in Scripture that reveals the purpose for Jesus' suffering as it relates to healing is Isaiah 53:4:

Surely He has borne our griefs (sicknesses, weaknesses, and distresses) and carried our sorrows and pains [of punishment] ... (AMPC)

The word *borne* in this verse means *to take, carry, or hold.* When Jesus was on the cross, He carried every form of sickness, weakness, pain, and disease on Himself.

That means cancer, lower back pain, skin issues, and even emotional issues like depression—He carried them all for you.

Of course, that doesn't mean we won't experience sickness or pain. But it does mean that when it shows up, we don't have to accept it as "normal."

We must be bold enough to know that whatever illness or problem we're currently facing, even if it's a result of our own bad decisions, did not come from God. Clearly God *cannot* be the source of sickness in your life, for the Bible says Jesus carried all sickness, weakness, and distress for you on the cross. He is the source of your healing!

Sickness is a result of the enemy's work and of living in this fallen world. But as a Believer, you have a right to stand boldly on God's promises for your healing and continued strength.

When sickness rears its ugly head and presses you with symptoms of any kind—whether it's a common cold, migraine headache, or something more serious—remind yourself that Jesus carried that affliction for you, and you don't have to keep it. Declare that He bore that weakness for you and speak out the victory that you've received!

GOD'S PROMISES

O LORD my God,

I cried to you for help,

and you restored my health.

(PSALM 30:2, NLT)

God, I call to You for help.

You are the One who has healed me in Christ and restores my health. I receive my healing from sickness now. I receive my strengthening from weakness now. I receive Your help in every area I need it.

The LORD will preserve him and keep him alive, and he will be blessed on the earth; You will not deliver him to the will of his enemies. The LORD will strengthen him on his bed of illness; You will sustain him on his sickbed. (Psalm 41:2–3, NKJV)

CONFESSION:

The Lord preserves me throughout the days of my life. He preserves my health, strength, and peace of mind. I am blessed. God will not allow the enemies of sickness, disease, or pain to win. He makes me strong and sustains me when I feel symptoms of sickness.

The Spirit of God, who raised Jesus from the dead, lives in you. And just as God raised Christ Jesus from the dead, he will give life to your mortal bodies by this same Spirit living within you. (Romans 8:11, NLT)

CONFESSION:

The Spirit of God lives inside of me. The same power that raised Jesus from the dead is alive in me. My body is quickened and strengthened by the Holy Spirit. I receive power from within to live whole, healthy, free, and strong.

HEALING NUGGETS

"I call You Healer
Your name is Healer
You are a Healer to me ...
Healer You are and healer You'll be"
—DONNIE MCCLURKIN

"Jesus is still in the healing business. The truth is many people need healing, but the doctors have no answer for it. There are still miracles today. There are still things that happen today you cannot explain other than the fact God did it."
—CHARLES STANLEY

"One of the ways Jesus referred to Himself was: The Physician. A physician is one who is skilled in the art of physical healing. We are three-part beings—spirit, soul, and body. Jesus is concerned about your physical body. He created it."
—ROBERT MORRIS

"When I was in the hospital, TBN was on cable television there. Your programming helped me to have hope. I was healed while watching the broadcasts. Now I am home, happy, and safe."

—ROY BALLWANZ JR., TBN PARTNER

CHAPTER 6

HEALING FOR BROKEN RELATIONSHIPS

God is a relational God.

Loving relationships are a cornerstone of life, the foundation of His church, and evidence that we have the love of God in our hearts. This is why God has invested so much into the health of our relationships.

If you're single, He's concerned about the health of your friendships and family relationships. If you're married, He's also concerned about the health of your marriage. Of course, He's also interested in the bond between parents and children and in how siblings relate to one another.

God places a big emphasis on how we relate to others because our relationships impact every area of our lives. We deal with people at work, at church, at school, and during everyday interactions like going to the grocery store.

From God's perspective, relationships are one of the primary ways the unsaved can see His love at work and discover a relationship with Him. Jesus said it like this in John 13:35: "Your love for one another will prove to the world that you are my disciples." (NLT)

This is why there are so many attacks against relationships. And when relationships break down, it impacts the quality of life. Unresolved bitterness and unforgiveness from relational wounds can be sources of sickness and even disease.

The wonderful thing is that God hasn't left us to figure things out for ourselves.

His Word is full of instructions for healing and maintaining healthy relationships. If you need healing and God's restorative touch in one of your relationships, allow God's Word to minister to you. Just like He wants you to be healed physically, He wants you to experience His healing touch in all of your relationships as well.

GOD'S PROMISES

Get rid of all bitterness,

rage, anger, harsh words, and

slander, as well as all types

of evil behavior. Instead,

be kind to each other,

tenderhearted, forgiving one

another, just as God through

Christ has forgiven you.

(EPHESIANS 4:31–32, NLT)

CONFESSION:

I walk in love.

Since God has forgiven me of all of my sins in Christ, I will not hold unforgiveness against anyone. I release all bitterness and anger. Lord, I pray peace over every misunderstanding and hurtful area in my relationships.

Hatred stirs up quarrels, but love makes up for all offenses. (Proverbs 10:12, NLT)

CONFESSION:

I am a person of peace and love. All strife is removed from my relationships. The love of God makes allowances for my mistakes as well as others. Understanding and selflessness govern my interactions with people in my family, at work, at church, and in every other area of my life.

Finally, all of you, be like-minded, be sympathetic, love one another, be compassionate and humble. Do not repay evil with evil or insult with insult. On the contrary, repay evil with blessing, because to this you were called so that you may inherit a blessing. For, "Whoever would love life and see good days must keep their tongue from evil and their lips from deceitful speech. They must turn from evil and do good; they must seek peace and pursue it." (1 Peter 3:8–11, NIV)

CONFESSION:

I do not repay others evil for any wrong they have done to me. I forgive them of their wrong, and I pray God's blessing on them. Father, I thank You for healing me from the insults and injuries I have suffered. You reward me with overflowing blessings as I walk in love. I love life. I see good days, because I speak life instead of death. I always seek out and live in the peace of God!

HEALING NUGGETS

"Forgiveness is one of the most self-loving things we'll ever do. Forgiveness doesn't make them right; it just makes us free."
—JIMMY EVANS

"Identify the fig leaves in your life—the things you use to try to cover up your nakedness. People struggle to get to a place of wholeness because, like Adam and Eve, they've sown fig leaves over the emotional trauma of bad breakups, relationship decisions, or things from the past. It's difficult to open up to love and trust when you have fig leaves everywhere."
—JOHN GRAY

"Relationships are complicated. It's complicated to bring two different people from different backgrounds together. Acknowledge the difficulty that comes with relationships in order to diffuse them. You can't always uncomplicate your life, but you can uncomplicate your approach to it."
—STEVEN FURTICK

"There was a woman who came to me for counseling whose husband was involved in an open affair. He'd come home in the evening, eat, and then change clothes and go spend the night with his girlfriend. Then he'd come home in the morning and change clothes, eat again, and then go to work.

"I told her, 'You don't have to stay in that relationship. If your husband is that flagrant and unwilling to change, I'm not asking you to stay in that relationship, and I don't believe God will either.'

"She said, 'Well, I love him, and I want my marriage to work.'

"I told her I wasn't forcing to her remain, but I said, 'This is what you should do if you want to fix your marriage. Ephesians 5 says to honor your husband as you would the Lord. I want you to go home and fix yourself up for your husband. Don't argue with him. Fix his favorite meal. Serve him. Love on him.'

"She said, 'Did you hear what I said about my husband?!'"
"I said, 'I told you, you can divorce him. But if you
want to redeem him, I'm telling you how to redeem
him. Go home and treat your husband like Jesus.'

"She came back the next week and said, 'I've got his
attention. He stays home longer and comes home earlier.
He's still spending the night with her, but I'm treating
him well, being affectionate, and we haven't argued.'
She said after the second or third night he asked
her, 'What's going on? What are you up to?' ...

"The next time she came in, he came with her. He said
to me, 'I know you know what I did! Well, she's treating
me great, and it's making me feel terrible! When she was
fighting with me, I'd spend the night with my girlfriend
and not feel bad about it. But now, I feel bad.'

"Long story short ... he got radically saved that day. He
became a member of church—fantastic husband, father. He's
now one of my favorite human beings! This is not always
the case. Sometimes relationships aren't redeemed. God will
bless and protect you when you are the redeemer. It may not
always work because of the choices other people can make
to change or not, but it always is the right way to live."
—JIMMY EVANS, TBN MINISTRY PARTNER

CHAPTER 7

HEALING FOR THE MIND

We are three part beings—

spirit, soul, and body. When we make Jesus the Lord of our lives, our spirit receives healing from spiritual death. But there are still two areas of our makeup that need Christ's healing touch—our souls (or our minds) and our physical bodies.

Inasmuch as Jesus healed people's bodies, He also healed their minds. In fact, God's Word teaches us that physical health and mental health are irrevocably linked.

Proverbs 23:7 says that as a man thinks in his heart, so is he. What we think about ourselves is inevitably what we become. Unhealthy thinking produces unhealthy living. Another verse of Scripture that highlights the connection between physical health and mental health is 3 John 1:2:

Beloved, I pray that you may prosper in all things and be in health, just as your soul prospers. (NKJV)

In that verse, note the phrase *"just as."* Other translations of the Bible, such as the King James Version, translate that phrase as *"even as."* In other words, our soul health has a direct correlation to physical health.

This is one of the reasons why God's Word places so much emphasis on a healthy thought life. God's Word is the avenue by which we can develop a healthy thought life. Scripture is the source of health for our thought life, because it is the only thing that can change our mind from unhealthy thought patterns that lead to unhealthy living.

For any area where our soul is sick—whether it be in low self-esteem, negative thoughts, or destructive habits—the Word of God is the answer to nourishing our minds into a balanced and healthy state.

The majority of the enemy's attacks begin in the mind. He uses wrong thoughts and images in our minds to try to get us to think in a way that will lead us away from God's best.

The only way to counteract this is to stand on God's promises and allow His healthy thoughts to permeate our thinking daily. Thoughts of fear can be replaced with thoughts of faith. Thoughts of lack can be replaced with thoughts of provision. And thoughts of failure and depression can be replaced with thoughts of success and joy.

GOD'S PROMISES

For though we walk in the flesh, we

do not war after the flesh: (For the

weapons of our warfare are not carnal,

but mighty through God to the pulling

down of strong holds;) Casting down

imaginations, and every high thing that

exalteth itself against the knowledge of

God, and bringing into captivity every

thought to the obedience of Christ.

(2 CORINTHIANS 10:3-5, KJV)

I win the battle of the mind.

God's Word and His promises are my weapons against wrong thought patterns and old ways of thinking. I cast down wrong imaginations and every thought that is in opposition to the Word of God.

Strip yourselves of your former nature [put off and discard your old unrenewed self] which characterized your previous manner of life and becomes corrupt through lusts and desires that spring from delusion; and be constantly renewed in the spirit of your mind [having a fresh mental and spiritual attitude], and put on the new nature (the regenerate self) created in God's image, [Godlike] in true righteousness and holiness.
(Ephesians 4:22–24, AMPC)

CONFESSION:

My mind is renewed by the Word of God. I allow His Word
to replace my old way of thinking and living. I have been
given right-standing with God and made holy in Christ;
I allow that nature to dominate my way of thinking.

Finally, brethren, whatsoever things are true, whatsoever
things are honest, whatsoever things are just, whatsoever things
are pure, whatsoever things are lovely, whatsoever things
are of good report; if there be any virtue, and if there be any
praise, think on these things. (Philippians 4:8, KJV)

CONFESSION:

I don't waste my time meditating on negative things.
I choose to think on the higher things of God. My
thought life is pure, honest, just, and lovely. My
mind focuses on virtuous things. Because my internal
thought life is focused on Him, my outward living
reflects the virtue, character, and nature of Christ.

HEALING NUGGETS

"Our mind tends to give us more trouble than anything. That's because the mind is the battlefield Satan comes and attacks us on. If you can win the battle in your mind, you can win the battle of life."
—JOYCE MEYER

"We can change our hair, our clothing, our address, our church, our spouse, or our residence. But if we don't change our mind, the same experience will perpetuate itself over and over again. Nothing is as powerful as a changed mind."
—T.D. JAKES

"Being a Christian is more than just an instantaneous conversion—it is a daily process whereby you grow to be more and more like Christ."
—BILLY GRAHAM

#MYSTORY

JESUS SOFTENS AN ANGRY MAN

"There was a lot of violence in my home while growing up. My mother was mentally ill, and she'd beat me severely all the time. As a result, violence and rage was all I knew. I tried to drown my pain in drugs, alcohol, and women. None of it worked.

"As result, in 1991 I was arrested and spent the next 24 years in prison. When you're doing a lot of prison time, it seems like an impossible task to find hope in such an environment.

"Then TBN's 2nd Chance program came along. It meant the world to me, because where I felt ashamed, guilty, and abandoned, TBN taught me about the love and mercy of God. In my weakness, they provided me a message that offered me strength.

"Being peaceful in such circumstances for as long as I was—that was the hardest thing I've ever had to do. The messages from TBN saved me. I exited prison knowing God loves me!"

—PAUL MARTIN, TBN PARTNER

CHAPTER 8

HEALING
FOR STRESS

Stress! It's so commonplace in our world.

The demands and responsibilities of life, the pace of modern society, and the uncertainty of the future can produce a great deal of hand-wringing. A mind focused on all the negativity will produce nothing but worry.

Jesus warned us in Matthew 6 not to worry about our lives because He knew we'd face constant temptation in this area. He warned His followers to not worry about what they'd eat or what they'd wear. Today, He'd admonish us to not worry about the same things—as well as our children's college fund, the faltering economy, or any number of daily bad news reports.

When we get lost in a lifestyle of worrying, our minds and bodies become overburdened with stress, unmercifully wearing us out under its pressure. Jesus knew that would happen, which is why He said in Matthew 6:31–33:

"So don't worry about these things, saying, 'What will we eat? What will we drink? What will we wear?' These things dominate the thoughts of unbelievers, but your heavenly Father already knows all your needs. Seek the Kingdom of God above all else, and live righteously, and he will give you everything you need." (NLT)

Yes! Our heavenly Father loves us and already knows everything we need. When we take hold of that truth, fear and doubt fall by the wayside.

Instead of meditating on our problems, we need to meditate on how big our God really is. When we keep our mind on our problems, we create anxiety and stress. But when we keep our mind on the promises of God, we create a lifestyle of peace.

Allow the promises of God to heal your soul of worry and stress by focusing on His goodness and willingness to show Himself *big* on your behalf today.

GOD'S PROMISES

"Are you tired? Worn out? Burned out on religion? Come to me. Get away with me and you'll recover your life. I'll show you how to take a real rest. Walk with me and work with me—watch how I do it. Learn the unforced rhythms of grace. I won't lay anything heavy or ill-fitting on you. Keep company with me and you'll learn to live freely and lightly."

(MATTHEW 11:28–30, MSG)

I draw close to Jesus ...

and enter into His rest. I am no longer dominated by stress and anxiety because Jesus teaches and shows me His grace. Daily time with Jesus causes me to live freely and peacefully.

Cast all your anxiety on him because he cares for you. (1 Peter 5:7, NIV)

CONFESSION:

I cast all my anxious thoughts on Jesus. He loves me. He's left nothing to chance. I don't have to carry the burdens of life on my back; God carries them for me. I trust Him and His Word to provide everything I need in life.

Don't worry about anything; instead, pray about everything. Tell God what you need, and thank him for all he has done. Then you will experience God's peace, which exceeds anything we can understand. His peace will guard your hearts and minds as you live in Christ Jesus. (Philippians 4:6–7, NLT)

CONFESSION:

I don't give in to needless worry. I pray about problems rather than complain about them. God hears my prayers, and I thank Him for all He has provided for me. I experience God's peace because I know He hears me and has already answered my prayers in Christ. I walk in the peace of Jesus Christ even under difficult circumstances … because God works on my behalf!

HEALING NUGGETS

"This is a time of great stress, and people are feeling it. They're turning to all kinds of means to eliminate it. They're looking for an escape. There is a solution God has provided for every one of His children: Solitude. Get alone with God!"
—CHARLES STANLEY

"Stress is your body's reaction to how you're thinking. Stress is simply the body's reaction to a foreign invasion of toxic thoughts. To address negative stress, you must address toxic thinking."
—DR. CAROLINE LEAF

"Whatever you meditate on is what you're giving a right to become a reality. When you worry and expect the worst, you invite the wrong things in your life. Quit inviting defeat, and use your faith to invite victory."
—JOEL OSTEEN

I cried out to the Lord like I did when I got saved. "If You're real, I need You to show up now." He did. He is so faithful.

"Taking care of her (my mom) was the hardest thing I've ever had to do. When she finally went home, I was lost. My mother was my core. She was the one who led me to the Lord—my example of Christ.

"Then my husband and I separated. I felt self-condemnation and condemnation from others because of my failure in my marriage. I was so stressed I didn't know what to do. I was alone. It was terrible and dark.

"I cried out to the Lord like I did when I got saved. 'If You're real, I need You to show up now.' He did. He is so faithful.

"I need to tell people: Out of pain, God does beautiful things. You can stand in your pain. Yes, it's natural to cry and mourn, but don't stay there. Move forward and help someone else."

—MARIA APONTE, TBN PARTNER

CHAPTER 9

HEALING FOR DEPRESSION

Jesus had a powerful instruction ...

for us in this world where tests, trials, and sorrows are guaranteed: "Take heart" (John 16:33, NLT). These words are more relevant now than ever with depression so common on the landscape of modern society.

When we are faced with hard times in this life, there are two choices. We can choose to give in to despair, or we can choose to take hold of joy.

So, what do we do when the world, filled with its onslaught of problems, draws our focus away from God and His promises? As He explained in John 16:33, NLT, Jesus provided a key to our escape:

"I have told you all this so that you may have peace in me. Here on earth you will have many trials and sorrows. But take heart, because I have overcome the world."

The key to not spiraling deep into depression—even when trials and sorrows come—is to return our focus to what Jesus has told us. It's remembering God's promises to us and taking heart! He has overcome the world ... and therefore, since we are *in Him* as Believers, we have done the same.

Everything we face, Jesus has already conquered. Depression, sorrow, and grief have no rule over us. The battle has been won. Instead of giving in to despair over the way things look to our natural eyes, Jesus wants us to focus our eyes on the world beyond our own. He wants us to remember the words He said.

In the comfort of those promises, we'll find lasting hope.

GOD'S
PROMISES

The LORD is close to the

brokenhearted; he rescues those

whose spirits are crushed.

(PSALM 34:18, NLT)

Even in my pain, Lord,

You are close to me. You are my rescuer in times of heaviness and sadness. Thank You for healing and strengthening me from within.

And God shall wipe away all tears from their eyes; and there shall be no more death, neither sorrow, nor crying, neither shall there be any more pain: for the former things are passed away. (Revelation 21:4, KJV)

CONFESSION:

Lord, I thank You that the pain of this life is temporary. Thank You for Your answers for every distressing issue I face. Thank You, Father, that I have an ultimate hope in Christ to be with You eternally where all earthly sorrow will be no more!

Why are you cast down, O my soul?
And why are you disquieted within me?
Hope in God;
For I shall yet praise Him,
The help of my countenance and my God.
(Psalm 43:5, NKJV)

CONFESSION:

God is the health and strength of my life. I put my hope in Him. Even when I feel sorrow and things look hopeless, I put my trust in the Lord. I am encouraged, helped, and strengthened in Christ. I praise Him, my Help!

HEALING NUGGETS

"We live in difficult times. Many have embraced this perpetual motif of failure or, in best cases, mere survival. That's not what God made you for. There's more for you in God. You will do nothing less than thrive."
—SAMUEL RODRIGUEZ

"There's an element of overcoming people often forget, and that is gratitude. Gratitude is what gets us through tough times. Gratitude matters to God."
—MAX LUCADO

"The darkness in this world is almost nonstop. How can you be joyful in a world that is anything but? My prayer is you awaken and realize this is the hour you were born for. The joy of the Lord is truly our strength, and we're not to draw back into depression."
—CHRISTINE CAINE

Someone taught
the Bible to
me so I could
understand
and apply it
to my life.

"I remember growing up in church, but I never had a relationship with God. I got introduced to marijuana when I was 13 years old. That led to harder drugs like cocaine and prescription pills. I kept getting worse and worse. My life spiraled out of control until I didn't want to live anymore.

"I found myself in the county detention center as a teenager, broken with no hope. My mom prayed for me to go to a teen rehabilitation center—Teen Challenge. They were going to send me to prison for four to six years. They gave me a choice. I could do that or go to Teen Challenge for a year. So that's what I did.

"I got delivered from drug addiction in a practical way. It wasn't a lightning bolt. It was going to a place that taught me how to pray and read the Word. I got discipled. Someone taught the Bible to me so I could understand and apply it to my life.

"I had a desire to change. I didn't want to live like that anymore. I worked with the Lord, and I think that's where my freedom came from."

—MARK ANTHONY, TBN PARTNER

CHAPTER 10

HEALING FOR GUILT, SHAME, AND CONDEMNATION

Unresolved guilt.
Shame. Condemnation.

They can be absolutely tormenting. Still, many Believers live bound with these feelings for years. These thieves unapologetically steal our rest and sap the joy out of life. But the pressure they put on our minds is undue—for God's forgiveness is greater than them all.

Jesus wants us to be confident in our right-standing with God, and in His forgiveness, because our health is often a reflection *of our perception* of our relationship with God. If we see ourselves as guilty, shamed, and condemned before God, we'll be tempted to shrink away from Him instead of running to Him to receive what we need. Ultimately, if we run, our health—physically, mentally, spiritually, even financially—will suffer.

Look at Jesus' message to us in Hebrews 4:15–16:

*This High Priest of ours understands our weaknesses, for he faced
all of the same testings we do, yet he did not sin. So let us come boldly
to the throne of our gracious God. There we will receive his mercy,
and we will find grace to help us when we need it most. (NLT)*

Jesus, your High Priest, is perfect and sinless. He understands,
and He is the reason why you can boldly draw near to
God. Never let feelings of guilt, shame, or condemnation
keep you from receiving all you need from Him.

You have been placed in perfect right-standing with
God. Remind yourself of this daily until you're confident
beyond a shadow of a doubt in who you are in Jesus.
Because that's the *only* way to be truly free!

GOD'S PROMISES

So now there is no

condemnation for those who

belong to Christ Jesus.

(ROMANS 8:1, NLT)

I am no longer condemned for my past mistakes.

Jesus took all of the condemnation and judgment for my sin on the cross. I am now in right-standing with God in Christ Jesus!

For the scripture saith, Whosoever believeth on him shall not be ashamed. (Romans 10:11, KJV)

I believe in Jesus Christ. I am never ashamed. He has accepted me, and now I have a healthy mindset concerning who I am … and whose I am. I am a new creation in Christ!

"Don't be afraid, for I am with you.
Don't be discouraged, for I am your God.
I will strengthen you and help you.
I will hold you up with my victorious right hand."
(Isaiah 41:10, NLT)

CONFESSION:

God upholds me with His victorious right hand. I am not afraid or discouraged. No matter what I face and encounter in this life, the Lord is with me. He strengthens me and causes me to remain solid, stable, free, and at peace. He is my is God, and I belong to Him.

HEALING NUGGETS

"Every human being is under construction
from conception to death."
—BILLY GRAHAM

"So many people carry shame. Everyone has a past.
Everyone has things they want to leave behind. Sin has a
wage, but grace grants a gift—the righteousness of God.
Through salvation there is freedom from shame."
—BRIAN HOUSTON

"Untreated guilt is the most fertile soil on the planet
for growing affliction. When you keep a messed-up
conscience, you are fertilizing affliction and trouble. The
enemy's trick is to keep you from going to God because
of guilt. If you have a guilty conscience, believe the
Word and draw near to God with a sincere heart."
—BETH MOORE

"The message I heard from the world, and even the church, was that I was a bad person. I was going to hell, and I needed to repent. I knew all of that was true. But what I really needed was some hope.

"I'll never forget my mother telling me my father had passed away from cancer. I felt hopeless and alone. It wasn't long after I was introduced to cocaine.

"My addictions spiraled out of control at 17. I came to the end of my rope at the age of 21. I stopped by my mom's house high on cocaine. She was there watching Christian television—TBN.

"I began to listen, and I heard this message that there's a God who loves me, cares for me, and wants to deliver me. I heard a message of hope. I knelt in my mother's living room that night and prayed to receive Christ!"

—SAL DIBIANCA, TBN PARTNER

CHAPTER 11

HEALING WHEN YOU'VE BEEN HURT

There are times in life ...

when we all experience rejection, betrayal, or overall disappointment. But if we hold on to those wounds, we can remain in a state of perpetual hurt. Many times it's not what happens to us, but how we *respond* to what happens that matters. If we respond in such a way that we allow the hurt to gain control of our thoughts, we can undermine our own emotional well-being.

Jesus doesn't want us to go through life carrying old wounds. He wants to heal us of past hurts. This is why He gave us the precious promises in His Word. Regardless of how badly we've been hurt, God *always* has our complete restoration on His mind.

Even if we've spent years wrestling with unresolved hurt, there is a way out. Psalm 147:3, NLT, says, "He heals the brokenhearted and bandages their wounds." When He was on Earth, Jesus was constantly healing people's pain and comforting them when they felt sorrow. And when He left Earth, He didn't leave us high and dry. He sent the *eternal* Source of comfort to live on the inside of each one of us—the Holy Spirit, who is our Comforter, Helper, and Friend.

The hurts you've experienced are real, but God doesn't want that to be your greatest reality. The Spirit of God is always with you and will never leave you. You can draw from His strength through every painful circumstance and find your healing.

Draw close to the Lord and allow Him to show you how the truth of His Word applies to the exact situation you're facing. Allow what He personally speaks to you to bring healing, understanding, and a sense of acceptance today.

GOD'S PROMISES

... I would not forget you!

See, I have written your name

on the palms of my hands.

(ISAIAH 49:15–16, NLT)

When people overlook me,

forget me, or take me for granted, I remember
I am always on God's mind. He has tattooed my
image on the palms of His hands. He's always
thinking about me, and that's what matters most.

*"I give you the authority ...
over all the power of the enemy,
and nothing shall by any means
hurt you."* (Luke 10:19, NKJV)

CONFESSION:

God has given me power through Jesus Christ. I have power over every attack against my emotions. Hurt emotions do not rule my life. Instead of focusing on what was done to me, I focus on the mighty power of God that is available in and through me.

"For the Lamb on the throne will be their Shepherd.
He will lead them to springs of life-giving water.
And God will wipe every tear from their eyes."
(Revelation 7:17, NLT)

CONFESSION:

Jesus sustains me, even in times of hurt and disappointment. He refreshes me when I'm in His presence. I drink of the living water of His Word and I am healed of all hurt.

HEALING
NUGGETS

"As you apply the truth of the Word of God to your
life, Jesus can heal you everywhere you hurt."
—CHRISTINE CAINE

"From the cross God declares, 'I love you. I know the heartaches
and the sorrows and the pain that you feel. But I love you.'"
—BILLY GRAHAM

"Scars are a testimony of God's ability to heal deadly wounds."
—JENTEZEN FRANKLIN

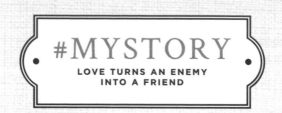

When you have
God, you're not
alone. I was
lost and upset.
Now that I let
God into my
life I'm happy.

"When I was in 6th grade I was bullied a lot.
It's hard because they say so many things about
you that aren't true, but it just gets to you.

"I would talk to my grandmother and, she would tell me to
pray to God. She recommended TBN a lot. This one day I
decided to put it on, and there was a show on talking about
everything I was dealing with and the drama at school.

"One day there, a bully was talking to me and telling me
I shouldn't be happy. I told her, 'I'm going to be happy no
matter what because I have God, and He's helping me. And
no matter what you say to me I'm going to pray for you.'

"She started to cry. She said that was the first
nice thing someone had said to her. I was
surprised. To this day we're friends.

"When you have God, you're not alone. I was lost and
upset. Now that I let God into my life I'm happy."
—MILISA PEREZ, TBN PARTNER

CHAPTER 12

HEALING FOR SOMEONE YOU LOVE

Life is about people and relationships.

This is why many times when a loved one needs healing, it can be just as pressing to us as if we were experiencing the pain ourselves. Because of the connection we have with those we love, when they hurt, we hurt.

One of the greatest things a Believer can do is to intercede in prayer on behalf of those who need healing. Whether it be a close family member or a distant friend, God can use each one of us to minister healing in someone else's life.

This principle is seen throughout Scripture.

- A centurion went to Jesus for healing on behalf of His servant (Matthew 8:5–6).
- A group of friends tore the roof off of a house to get their friend into Jesus' presence so he could be healed of palsy (Mark 2:1–5).
- A concerned father went to Jesus for healing when his daughter was at the point of death (Mark 5:22–23).

The Bible says we have the ability to bless or curse with our words. When we take the time to pray the Word of God over a loved one, we are speaking God's blessings over them. When we unselfishly pray His promises over the hurting, we are counteracting the curse.

Take the time to purposefully pray for your family, coworkers, friends, and even strangers. You will become a vessel of love that God can flow His goodness through to touch others ... a vessel that changes the world!

GOD'S
PROMISES

... pray for one another, that you

may be healed and restored. The

heartfelt and persistent prayer

of a righteous man (believer)

can accomplish much [when put

into action and made effective

by God—it is dynamic and can

have tremendous power].

(JAMES 5:16, AMP)

I am the righteousness of God in Christ.

Therefore, my prayers for others are dynamic and powerful. I thank God His ears are open to my prayers. I speak physical and emotional health over my family, friends, coworkers, acquaintances, and the lost.

"They will be able to place their hands on the sick, and they will be healed." (Mark 16:18, NLT)

CONFESSION:

I operate as a Believer in this Earth with Jesus' endorsement.
I have the ability to pray and lay hands on the sick and to
see them recover because the Spirit of God lives in me!

Pray in the Spirit at all times and on every occasion.
Stay alert and be persistent in your prayers for all
believers everywhere. (Ephesians 6:18, NLT)

CONFESSION:

I submit to God's instruction to pray for my brothers and
sisters in the body of Christ. I speak blessing, healing,
deliverance, and favor over others. I am a blessing to them!
God uses me mightily to bring healing into other people's lives.

HEALING NUGGETS

"Dignity is not a fruit of the spirit. Jesus said you have to be willing to look like a fool because God confounds the wise. Instead of asking yourself what if the person you pray for doesn't get healed, ask yourself what if they do get healed?"
—TODD WHITE

"The most eloquent prayer is the prayer through hands that heal and bless."
—BILLY GRAHAM

"The New Testament assures us that the fervent prayers of righteous men can make a difference."
—DAVID JEREMIAH

#MYSTORY

**INTECESSORY PRAYER HEALED HER
DEPRESSION AND SUICIDAL THOUGHTS**

"Leilee, from Iran, suffered from depression. She told us how she was praying to God nonstop for her condition. She told us she was going to end her life, and even explained how she was going to do it. However, before she had the chance, she came across our television network, TBN Nejat TV. She stopped what she was doing and immediately called us.

"Our prayer counselors started to pray with her and explained to her that Jesus loves her and that she needs to believe in Him and never stop trusting in His healing power. After talking with her a while she felt much better—we told her to stay in touch with us and to continue watching Nejat.

"Eventually she called back to tell us that she has started reading the Bible, is still watching our network, and that knowing that someone is praying for her has helped her understand how much Jesus loves her.

"Praise the Lord, she sounded much better and happier! She told us that she stopped taking medication and that she has plans to introduce Jesus to the people who have the same condition."
—TBN NEJAT PRAYER COUNSELOR